Red Parrot, Green Parrot

Tunes, songs and games for young string players
by
Edward Huws Jones

PUPIL'S BOOK (VIOLIN)

FABER *ff* MUSIC

Contents

© 1990 by Faber Music Ltd

First published in 1990 by Faber Music Ltd

Bloomsbury House 74–77 Great Russell Street London WC1B 3DA

Illustrations by John Levers

Cover design by M & S Tucker

Printed in England by Caligraving Ltd

ISBN10: 0-571-51171-6

EAN13: 978-0-571-51171-6

1 Tick Tock Clock

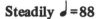

Tick tock, tick tock, tick tock, tick tock,

etc.

and stop!

2 Hurdy-Gurdy

3 Seagull

Expansively ♩=84

mp

Sea - gull, sea - gull, swoop and soar,

5

FINE

8 D.C. al FINE

from the o - cean to the shore.

Pupil makes free,
flowing movements
of the bow in the air.

4 Giant Footsteps

Heavily ♩=72

Hear the gi - ant foot - steps, hear the gi - ant foot - steps,

shake the doors and shake the win - dows, HEAR THE GI - ANT FOOT - STEPS!

5 Goblin Cobbler

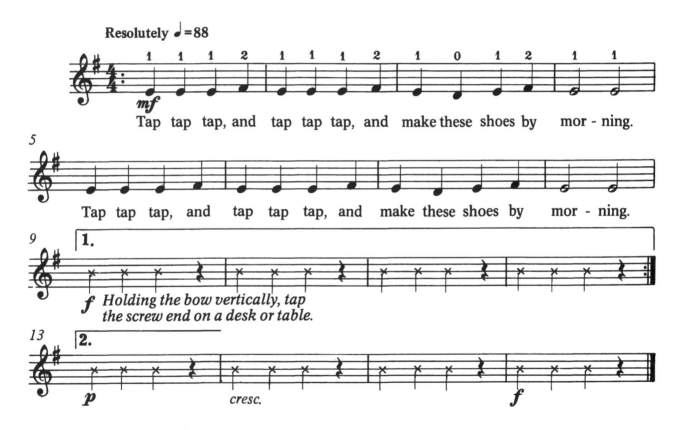

6 Red Parrot, Green Parrot

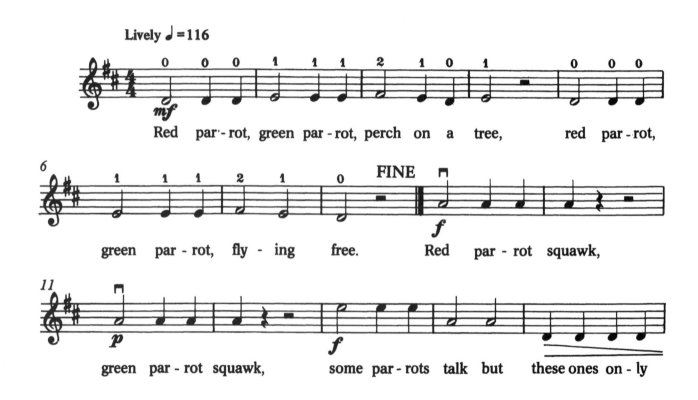

Red par-rot, green par-rot, perch on a tree, red par-rot,

green par-rot, fly-ing free. Red par-rot squawk,

green par-rot squawk, some par-rots talk but these ones on-ly

7 Gideon was a Soldier

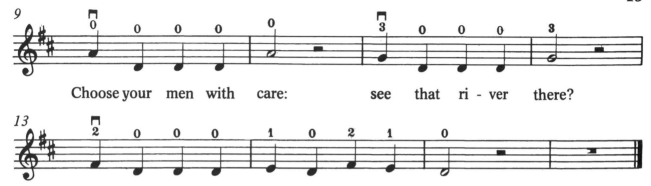

Choose your men with care: see that ri - ver there?

Those who drop their swords to drink don't fight.'

2 That left just three hundred,
   Gideon was outnumbered
   But the Lord said 'Trust in me!
   Wait until it's night,
   We'll give them a fright,
   We're the champions,
      Just you wait and see.'

3 Flaming brands were hid in
   Jars, as they were bidden,
   Gideon and the chosen few;
   Right up close they crept
   (Midianites just slept),
   Broke the jars,
      and beat them black and blue.

8 Skating

9 *Where's my Wellies?*

Rain is rain - ing, wind is blow - 'ing, pud - dles grow - ing,

where's my wel - lies? Rain is rain - ing, wind is blow - ing, soon it will be

10 Climbing

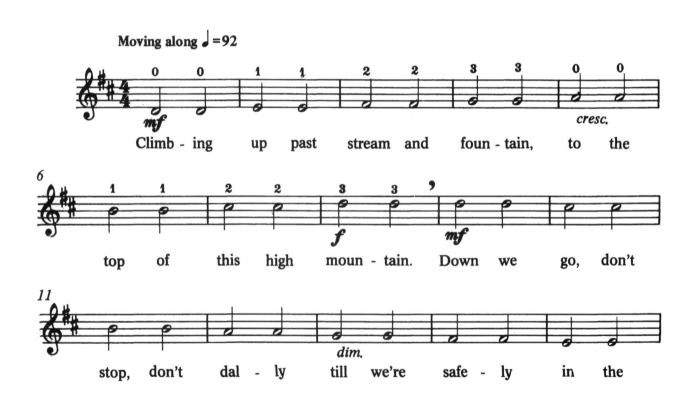

Climb - ing   up   past   stream   and   foun - tain,   to   the

top   of   this   high   moun - tain.   Down   we   go,   don't

stop,   don't   dal - ly   till   we're   safe - ly   in   the

val - ley. Now it's ea - sy,

run to the top; waltz down

a - gain be - fore we drop.

11 Passamezzo

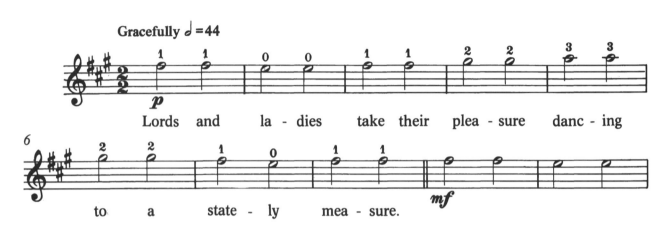

Gracefully ♩=44

p

Lords and la - dies take their plea - sure danc - ing

to a state - ly mea - sure.

mf

12 Three Fat Pussy Cats

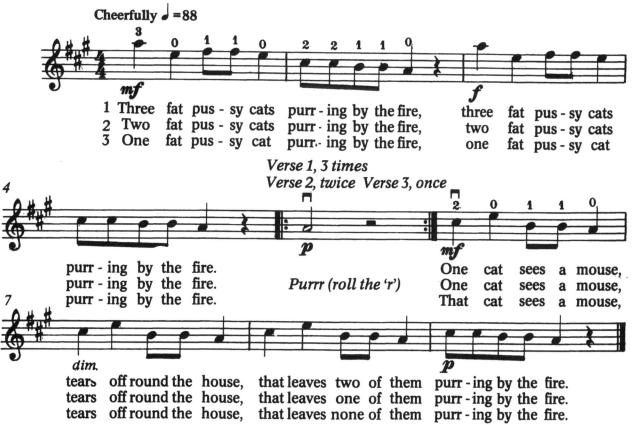

13 Hallowe'en

Creepy ♩=80

Who's that? black cat? big bat?
COME TO GET YOU! Mid - night, cats fight,
bats bite, HERE THEY COME!

Screams, caterwauls and bat squeaks –
bow behind the bridge.

Sun - rise,   cats' eyes,   bat   flies,   *SH!* ___

14 Want to Ride my Steam Train?

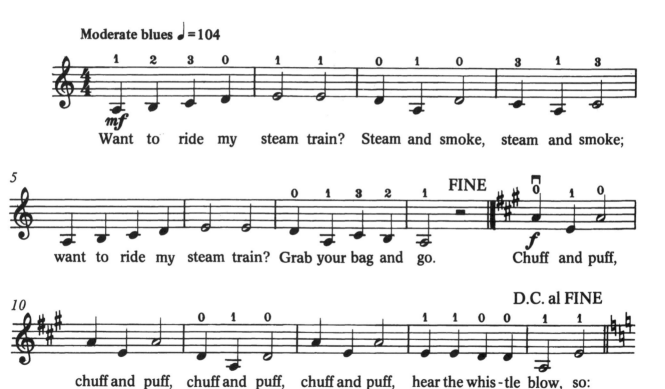

15 Michaelmas Moon

Moon shi·ning, mist ri-sing, eve-ning light. Dew fall-ing,

owl call-ing, au-tumn night.

16 Marching Band

March tempo ♩=96

March - ing, we're march - ing, the bu - gles blow, it's time to go, we're

march - ing, we're march - ing, the trum - pets play, we're on our way.

Left, *two, three, four,* left, *two, three, four,* left, left, left right, left right.

Left, *two, three, four,* left, *two, three, four,* left, left, left right, left right.

D.C. al FINE

Printed and bound in Great Britain by Caligraving Limited